A TRUE BOOK

Simple Machines

DANA MEACHEN RAU

Children's Press®
An Imprint of Scholastic Inc.
New York   Toronto   London   Auckland   Sydney
Mexico City   New Delhi   Hong Kong
Danbury, Connecticut

Content Consultant
Suzanne E. Willis
Professor and Assistant Chair, Department of Physics
Northern Illinois University
DeKalb, Illinois

Library of Congress Cataloging-in-Publication Data

Rau, Dana Meachen, 1971–
  Simple machines / Dana Meachen Rau.
     p. cm. — (A true book)
  Includes bibliographical references and index.
  ISBN-13: 978-0-531-26324-2 (lib. bdg.)   ISBN-13: 978-0-531-26586-4 (pbk.)
  ISBN-10: 0-531-26324-x (lib. bdg.)   ISBN-10: 0-531-26586-2 (pbk.)
  1. Simple machines—Juvenile literature. I. Title. II. Series.
  TJ147.R359 2011
  621.8—dc22   2011007506

All rights reserved. Published in 2012 by Children's Press, an imprint of Scholastic Inc.
Printed in China 62
SCHOLASTIC, CHILDREN'S PRESS, A TRUE BOOK, and associated logos are trademarks and/or registered trademarks of Scholastic Inc.
1 2 3 4 5 6 7 8 9 10 R 21 20 19 18 17 16 15 14 13 12

Find the Truth!

Everything you are about to read is true **_except_** for one of the sentences on this page.

Which one is **TRUE**?

T or F   Simple machines help us do less work.

T or F   Your teeth are simple machines.

Find the answers in this book.

Contents

THE **BIG** TRUTH!

So Many Simple Machines!

A wedge pencil sharpener

4 Ramp It Up

How do inclined planes help raise objects higher?

5 Break Apart and Hold Together

How do wedges and screws convert forces?

William Painter invented the bottle cap and bottle opener in the late 1800s.

Bicycles are made from a combination of simple machines.

6

Easy Does It

The world is filled with machines that make our lives easier. You use a refrigerator to keep food cold and a computer to help you with homework. These machines are run by electrical power. You use your own power to run machines, too. You power your bicycle to get where you need to go. Did you know that when you open a door, you are powering a machine?

 The term "bicycle" was first used in 1863.

The Simplest Machines

Simple machines are devices with very few parts that help us move objects. There are six simple machines: the wheel and **axle,** the lever, the pulley, the inclined **plane,** the wedge, and the screw.

A **force** is a push or a pull. Forces move objects. Simple machines make this job easier. They change the amount of the force or the direction of the force needed to move that object.

A boat paddle is a kind of lever.

About 90 percent of a pumpkin's weight is water.

Friction and gravity make it hard to move heavy objects.

The Forces Against You

You may have to work against **gravity** and **friction** to get something to move. Gravity is the force of two objects pulling on each other. Objects have weight because of Earth's gravity. Friction is the force of two objects rubbing against each other. If you drop a pencil, it may roll far on a wood floor. If you drop it on a thick rug, however, the pencil soon comes to a stop. There's more friction between the pencil and the rug than between the pencil and the floor.

Mechanical Advantage

Do you have a lot of work to do? Scientists don't use the word *work* to mean a lot of spelling or math. In science, work refers to the force that acts on an object to move it over a certain distance. Scientists do this math problem to find out how much work has been done to move an object:

Work = Force x Distance

It takes a lot of work to lift a heavy backpack.

You do work when you apply a force to push or pull a simple machine. If you get more force out of the machine than you put into it, that machine has a **mechanical advantage**. The mechanical advantage is how many times the machine multiplies the force. In other words:

*Mechanical Advantage = **Output** Force ÷ **Input** Force*

One square foot (0.1 square meters) of snow can weigh up to 20 pounds (9 kilograms)!

A shovel uses mechanical advantage to help a person lift heavy snow.

For example, if your input force is 1 and your output force is 5, then the mechanical advantage of that machine is 5. This means that the machine makes your work five times easier.

Mechanical Advantage = Output Force ÷ Input Force

Mechanical Advantage = 5 ÷ 1

Mechanical Advantage = 5

Wheels and levers work to increase a dolly's mechanical advantage.

A crutch
is a kind
of lever.

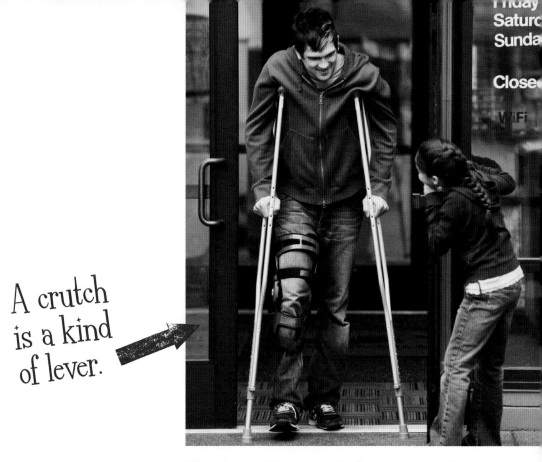

Simple machines can help someone who is injured move around.

Simple machines make work easier because you can use less force to move an object than if you didn't have the machine. You still need to do the same amount of work to get the job done. But you can spread that work over a longer distance. This means you don't have to do all the work at once.

Very large dump trucks are used by mining companies to carry the gold, coal, or other mined substances.

CHAPTER 2

Getting Around

The wheel is one of the most important discoveries of all time. Before the wheel was invented, people had to push or drag heavy objects. When wheels were created, people could use carts and wagons to carry their loads. Today, we use wheels on trucks, cars, and buses. They help us move heavy loads and people over long distances.

The earliest record of a wheel dates back to about 3500 B.C.E.

Wheels and Axles

Ancient civilizations built cities out of stone. Heavy stone blocks were moved by placing logs underneath them. The blocks could roll more easily on the logs than on the ground. The logs worked like wheels. Try this using some crayons. Line five of them up on a table. Place the crayon box on top of them. Can you move the box across the table using the crayons like wheels?

Ancient Egyptians used simple machines to help them move heavy stones for the pyramids.

Egyptians built pyramids to hold the bodies of their dead leaders.

Larger bike wheels cover more distance with one turn than smaller bike wheels.

Look at the bottom of a skateboard. Each set of wheels is attached to a thin bar called an axle. When this axle makes one complete turn, so do the wheels. The size of the wheels increases its mechanical advantage. If a skateboard's wheels make one complete turn, the skateboard moves a few inches. If a car's wheels make one turn, the car may move a few feet. The axle just needs to turn once. The larger wheels travel a longer distance in one rotation.

Wheels also make work easier by cutting down on friction. It is easier to roll your backpack across the floor on a skateboard than it is to drag it without one. The wheels change the amount of force needed to move the object.

The size and hardness of skateboard wheels affect how fast you travel.

Skateboards were invented by surfers who wanted to practice when they weren't around water.

Water Power

For hundreds of years, people used the power of rivers to turn large wooden waterwheels. Moving water pushed on the blades of the wheel. This turned an axle inside the mill. The axle moved parts on machines that ground grain into flour.

Sails are usually shaped like squares or triangles.

Sailors use pulleys to raise and lower sails.

Pulleys

Sailors hurry to raise their ship's sail when the wind blows. They pull down on the rope of a pulley to lift up a sail. That's a lot easier than climbing the mast and raising the sail by hand.

A pulley is a wheel with a groove around its edges. A rope or cord is threaded through the groove. Pulleys change the direction of a force. Instead of pulling up to lift an object, you need to pull down. That makes it easier to lift heavy objects.

There is no mechanical advantage to using a single pulley. Your pulling force is equal to the force that lifts the object. The pulley just changes the direction of the force, which makes the job easier.

Lots of pulleys working together, however, can help lessen the force you need to use and give you a mechanical advantage. More rope is needed, so the work is spread out over a longer distance.

Cranes use pulleys to lift heavy loads.

Catapults, a type of lever,
were important weapons
in Europe during the
Middle Ages.

CHAPTER 3

Lift and Lower

In the Middle Ages, catapults shot rocks into castle walls. A catapult is really a huge lever. A simple lever is a long rod or board that moves on a fixed point called a **fulcrum**. The load is the object you need to lift. The effort is the force you use on the lever.

Some catapults were designed to shoot arrows or spears at enemies during battle.

Fulcrum, Load, and Effort

All levers have a fulcrum, load, and effort. You can change the mechanical advantage of a lever by moving the position of the fulcrum. If you move the fulcrum closer to your load, you can use less force to move the load. But you'll have to apply that force over a greater distance.

Levers are helpful for changing tires.

The lever used to loosen bolts on a car's wheel is called a tire iron.

You use a lever when you play on a seesaw.

The order of the fulcrum, load, and effort determines what kind of lever you have. In a first class lever, the fulcrum is between the load and the effort. A seesaw is a first class lever. So is a crowbar. In this type of lever, the effort pushes down for the load to go up. Like a pulley, this simple machine changes the direction of the force needed to move an object.

Moving Together

In second and third class levers, both the effort and the load move in the same direction. The load is between the fulcrum and the effort in a second class lever. When you lift it, your load lifts, too. For example, when you lift a bottle opener, the cap comes up. When you lift a wheelbarrow, you lift the materials in the wheelbarrow, too.

A bottle opener is just one of the many useful levers commonly found in people's homes.

The first World Series was played in 1903. ➤

A baseball bat might not seem like a lever until you notice how it hits a baseball.

In a third class lever, the effort is between the fulcrum and the load. When you swing a baseball bat, you are using a third class lever. The fulcrum is the base or handle, of the bat. The effort is your hand pushing it forward to swing. The load is the ball that you send flying over the fence.

So Many Simple Machines!

Amusement parks are filled with fun. But did you know that they are also filled with simple machines? Next time you are at an amusement park take a look around. What simple machines can you spot? Here are a few to get you started.

You need inclined planes to zoom down roller coaster hills!

Pulleys make the flags fly high.

Some rides, like the pirate ship, are levers.

A winding waterslide is a screw shape.

The Ferris wheel is a big wheel and axle.

The plastic forks and knives at the snack bar are wedges.

Ramps make it easier to lift heavy objects.

CHAPTER 4

Ramp It Up

Wheels make it easy to push a grocery cart on flat ground. What if there is a step up to get into the store? You might need help lifting the cart to the higher level. A ramp would make this job easier. A ramp covers a longer distance than a step. But it is a lot easier to roll the cart up a ramp than to lift it up a step.

 Many moving trucks have built-in ramps.

Inclined Planes

When scientists talk about a plane, they mean a flat surface. An inclined plane is a flat surface that is slanted. A wheelchair ramp is an inclined plane. Inclined planes make it easier to move objects to a higher level.

As you push an object up a ramp, gravity pulls it down. The steeper the ramp, the harder it is to push an object up. The longer the distance the ramp covers, the less steep it will be.

 The first known wheelchair was built in 1595 for King Philip II of Spain.

People in wheelchairs use ramps to enter and exit buildings.

Long Distance

Is it worth it to push an object over a longer distance? Yes! A long inclined plane gives you a mechanical advantage. You can use less force to move your object. That will make your job easier.

A hill and a slide are inclined planes. A staircase, even though it has steps, is also an inclined plane. Imagine climbing up a straight ladder to get to the second floor. Stairs make that job a lot easier.

You use an inclined plane when you speed down a waterpark slide.

The wedge shape of an axe splits the log apart.

CHAPTER 5

Break Apart and Hold Together

A lumberjack chops down a tree with an axe. The wedge of the axe head makes a crack in the trunk. The axe cuts in deeper when he strikes the trunk again. Eventually, the trunk breaks apart. A wedge is shaped like an inclined plane. Unlike an inclined plane, however, the wedge is the object that moves. Wedges are used to break things apart or hold them together.

Each year, the Lumberjack World Championships are held in Wisconsin.

Converting Forces

Early people used stone wedges such as knives, axes, and other cutting tools. Farmers used plows to break up the soil. We still use these wedges today. You even have a set of wedges in your mouth. You use your teeth to break apart food.

Teeth are hard on the outside, but the insides are softer, living tissue.

You use simple machines every time you eat, because your teeth are simple machines.

A wedge makes work easier because it **converts** force from one direction to another. A force pushes the wedge straight into an object. The wedge then converts that forward force into two sideways forces. This helps push objects apart, like when an axe cuts a log.

Friction helps a wedge hold objects together. A doorstop tightly wedged between the door and the floor keeps the door open.

Notice that a doorstop has the same shape as an axe.

Screws

If you were tiny, you could slide down the thread of a screw from the top to the bottom. A screw is really just one long inclined plane wrapped around a center post. The distance between the threads is called the **pitch**.

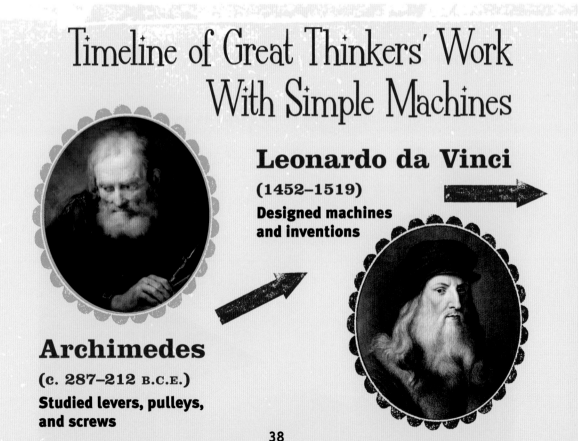

Timeline of Great Thinkers' Work With Simple Machines

Leonardo da Vinci
(1452–1519)
Designed machines and inventions

Archimedes
(c. 287–212 B.C.E.)
Studied levers, pulleys, and screws

Screws hold objects together. One example is a pickle jar and its lid.

Screws can also help apply more force to an object. A woodworker's vise squeezing together two pieces of wood is an example of this.

Galileo

(1564–1642)

Experimented with gravity and movement

Isaac Newton

(1642–1727)

Defined the three laws of how objects move

Many scholars believe that the screw was invented more than 2,500 years ago by a man named Archytas of Tarentum.

Like a wedge, a screw also converts forces. You turn the top of a screw with a screwdriver in a circular motion. The screw changes this circular motion into an upward or downward motion. The direction depends on which way you turn the screw.

Archimedes' Screw

Archimedes was a Greek mathematician who lived more than 2,000 years ago. He invented a device that could raise water from a low to a high area. This long screw was sealed inside a cylinder and placed on a slant in a body of water. A crank turned the screw and lifted the water up the cylinder until it reached the top. The screw could be used to water farmland or drain flooded areas.

Archimedes' screw is still used in some parts of the world.

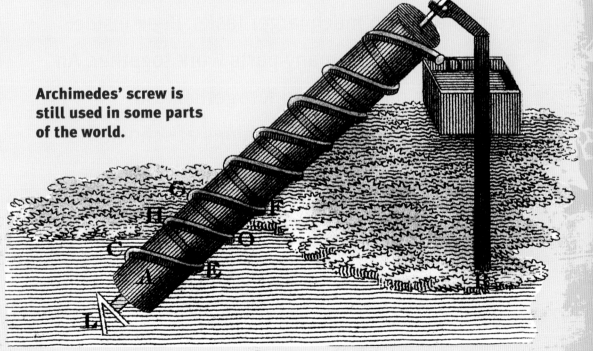

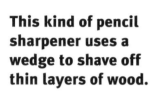

Pencil lead is made of clay and graphite.

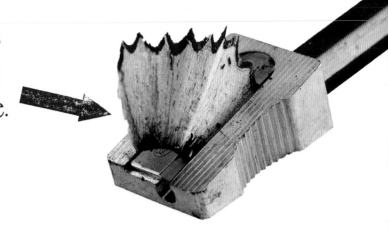

This kind of pencil sharpener uses a wedge to shave off thin layers of wood.

Simple Machines Today

The basic jobs of simple machines can be combined to do much larger tasks. Peek inside a clock to see how many parts work together. An engine has parts that work together, too.

Think about simple machines at school. Did the wheels on the bus bring you there? Maybe your teacher stores his or her supplies in cabinets with levers for doors. You can sharpen your pencil with the wedge inside the pencil sharpener.

Simplify your life with simple machines! ★

World's tallest roller coaster: Kingda Ka at Six Flags in New Jersey, at 418 ft. (127.4 m)

Longest home run ever hit in Major League Baseball: 575 ft. (175.3 m)

Weight of world's largest axe: More than 110,000 lbs. (49,895 kg)

Highest skateboard jump off of a ramp: 23.5 ft. (7.2 m)

Longest distance a pumpkin has ever been catapulted: 3,755.7 ft. (1,144.7 m)

When Archimedes' screw was invented: Third century B.C.E.

Did you find the truth?

F Simple machines help us do less work.

T Your teeth are simple machines.

Resources

Books

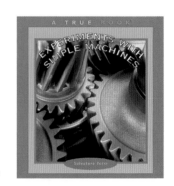

Bradley, Kimberly Brubaker. *Forces Make Things Move*. New York: HarperCollins, 2005.

Gardner, Robert. *Sensational Science Projects With Simple Machines*. Berkeley Heights, NJ: Enslow Elementary, 2006.

Nankivell-Aston, Sally. *Science Experiments With Simple Machines*. New York: Franklin Watts, 2000.

Oxlade, Chris. *Wheels*. North Mankato, MN: Smart Apple Media, 2007.

Richards, Jon. *Forces and Simple Machines*. New York: PowerKids Press, 2008.

Silverman, Buffy. *Simple Machines: Forces in Action*. Chicago: Heinemann Library, 2009.

Thompson, Gare. *Lever, Screw, and Inclined Plane: The Power of Simple Machines*. Washington, DC: National Geographic, 2006.

Tocci, Salvatore. *Experiments With Simple Machines*. New York: Children's Press, 2003.

Walker, Sally M. *Work*. Minneapolis: Lerner Publications, 2002.

Organizations and Web Sites

Amusement Park Physics

www.learner.org/interactives/parkphysics/index.html

Read about how physics plays a part in the way amusement park rides move, spin, and twist.

The Franklin Institute: Resources for Science Learning

http://sln.fi.edu/qa97/spotlight3/spotlight3.html

Explore the types of simple machines, with descriptions and details about how they work.

Museum of Science and Industry: Simple Machines Game

www.msichicago.org/online-science/simple-machines
/activities/simple-machines-1

Use your knowledge of simple machines to play this game and learn more about how planes and other machines work.

Places to Visit

Exploratorium

At the Palace of Fine Arts
3601 Lyon Street
San Francisco, CA 94123
(415) 561-0360
www.exploratorium.edu
Visit hundreds of exhibits to learn about science in our complex world.

Museum of Science

1 Science Park
Boston, MA 02114
(617) 723-2500
www.mos.org
Explore nature, technology, physics, and space in this vast museum.

Important Words

axle (AK-suhl)—a rod in the center of a wheel, around which the wheel turns

converts (kuhn-VURTS)—turns something into something else

force (FORS)—any action that produces, stops, or changes the shape or the movement of an object

friction (FRIK-shuhn)—the force that slows down objects when they rub against each other

fulcrum (FUL-kruhm)—the point on which a lever rests or turns

gravity (GRAV-i-tee)—the force that pulls things toward the center of the earth and keeps them from floating

input (IN-put) something that is put in

mechanical advantage (muh-KAN-i-kuhl uhd-VAN-tij)—a measure of the additional force gained by using a simple machine to do work

output (OUT-put) the amount of something that a machine produces

pitch (PICH)—the distance between the threads on a screw

plane (PLAYN)—a flat surface

Index

Page numbers in **bold** indicate illustrations

About the Author

Dana Meachen Rau is the author of more than 275 books for children. A graduate of Trinity College in Hartford, Connecticut, she has written fiction and nonfiction titles covering early readers, science, history, cooking, and many other topics that interest her. Her curiosity about how the world works made this book especially interesting to write. Now she can't help noticing simple machines everywhere she goes. Dana lives with her family in Burlington, Connecticut. To learn more about her books, please visit www.danameachenrau.com.

PHOTOGRAPHS © 2012: Alamy Images: 25 (amana images inc.), 17 (Peter Cavanagh), 34 (Ted Foxx), 30 (David R. Frazier Photolibrary, Inc.), 21 (Leslie Garland Picture Library), 29 right (Alan Look), 28 (Oleksiy Maksymenko Photography), 19 (Willy Matheisl), 29 top (Nordicphotos), 38 right, 39 left (North Wind Picture Archives), 32 (Photofusion Picture Library), 9 (RVN_), 38 left (The Art Gallery Collection), 41 (The Print Collector), 29 center bottom (Peter M. Wilson); Aurora Photos/Kim's Photo: cover; Dana Meachen Rau: 48; Dreamstime.com/James Phelps Jr./Mandj98: back cover; Getty Images/Imagno/Hulton Archive: 39 right; iStockphoto: 18 (Galina Barskaya), 37 (Rob Cruse), 33 (Laurentiu Iordache), 22 (Rafael Laguillo); Media Bakery: 12 (Phil Boorman), 20 (Henglein/Steets), 36 (Jose Luis Pelaez), 13 (Anderson Ross), 8 (Ariel Skelley/Blend Images), 24 (Somos), 3, 27, 29 center top; National Geographic Stock/H.M. Herget: 16; Photo Researchers, NY/CC Studio: 10, 43; Scholastic Library Publishing, Inc.: 44; ShutterStock, Inc.: 40 (afitz), 4 (M. Dykstra), 14 (kaband), 5 bottom, 26 (Picsfive), 29 bottom (STILLFX), 11 (Yun Yulia); Wikimedia Commons: 6 (C. Corleis), 5 top, 42 (Alexander Klink).